YOU ARE THE UNION

AWAKENING WHOLENESS THROUGH SHIVA–SHAKTI CONSCIOUSNESS

PUJA SINHA

Clever Fox®
PUBLISHING

Chennai • Bangalore

CLEVER FOX PUBLISHING
Chennai, India

Published by CLEVER FOX PUBLISHING 2026

ISBN: 978-93-7500-628-2

CONTENTS

ABOUT THE AUTHOR

Puja Sinha — guided by her passion for spiritual exploration — opens the path to the union of Shiva and Shakti.

Her *work blends empathy, storytelling, and practical exercises — guiding readers to not only understand spiritual concepts but to embody them in relationships, healing, and daily living. Puja's writing is marked by warmth and clarity, inviting readers into a journey of remembrance: to rediscover the wholeness, balance, and authenticity that already lives within them. She believes that spirituality is not separate from modern life — it is woven into our relationships, careers, and personal growth.*

Through her book You Are the Union: Awakening Wholeness Through Shiva–Shakti Consciousness, Puja offers a homecoming — guiding readers to restore balance, heal emotional wounds, and reconnect with their soul's original blueprint.

INTRODUCTION

In the vast tapestry of spiritual wisdom, few principles are as profound and universal as the ideology of Shiva–Shakti. This divine union represents the foundation of existence itself — the interplay of pure consciousness (Shiva) and dynamic energy (Shakti). In the ancient traditions of Tantra, Yoga, and Sanātana Dharma, this sacred duality explains not only the creation of the cosmos but also the deepest workings of the human mind, energy, and relationships.

Today's generation actively seeks meaning, balance, and purpose. In a world filled with distraction, uncertainty, and ego-driven pursuits, the Shiva–Shakti teachings serve as a guiding light. They help us understand our internal energies, heal emotional wounds, manifest our desires, and align with our higher selves.

This book is a journey through this ancient wisdom — a modern spiritual guide for inner harmony, conscious relationships, and awakened living.

Why Shakti Comes First

Shakti is often named before Shiva because energy precedes form. Shakti is the cosmic force, the movement, the power that animates existence. Without Shakti, Shiva remains pure potential, still and inactive. This is why scriptures declare: "Shiva without Shakti is shava" — a corpse. It is only through Shakti that consciousness becomes creation.

What This Book Offers

This book is not just knowledge — it is a mirror, a guide, and a remembrance. It awakens the union of Shiva and Shakti within you, showing how every challenge, relationship, and pause is a doorway to wholeness.

You will discover:

- **The Birth of Duality** — why awareness begins with Shakti's first dance.
- **Beyond Ego** — how calmness dissolves resistance and awakens Shakti.
- **Energy Beyond Gender** — the Divine Feminine and Masculine within.
- **Twin Flames & Manifestation** — how relationships and balance shape creation.
- **Healing & Integration** — turning wounds into wisdom and harmony.
- **Soul Growth & Surrender** — the art of letting go and trusting.
- **Karmic Lessons & Alignment** — how pain, contracts, and timing guide your path.

What this book truly offers is remembrance, that your wounds are teachers, your relationships are mirrors, your pauses are blessings, and your purpose has always lived within you.

Above all, it offers a homecoming — the realization that **you are the union, the wholeness, the living dance of Shiva and Shakti.**

PART 1

CHAPTER 1

(THE COSMIC BEGINNING - BIRTH OF DUALITY)

Before anything ever existed — before the first star burned, before space stretched, before time even began to move — there was only **one presence**, an infinite field of pure awareness. This presence was not lonely, nor was it waiting. It simply *was*. This eternal stillness is what ancient sages called **Shiva**.

Shiva is the unchanging witness, the quiet centre of all existence. Imagine the calm of an ocean so deep that no wave ever touches its floor — that depth is Shiva. Millions today feel disconnected from this state, not realizing that silence is not emptiness but the **origin of all creation**.

The First Movement: The Emergence of Shakti

From this infinite stillness came a single tremor — a vibration like the soft hum before music begins. This vibration was **Shakti**, the first breath of the cosmos. If Shiva is the ocean, Shakti is the wave. If Shiva is thought, Shakti is the feeling behind it. If Shiva is potential, Shakti is expression.

The sages say that Shakti did not "arrive" from outside Shiva, but blossomed from within him. She was his own power, his own heartbeat, his own desire to know himself through creation. Without her, Shiva remained unmanifest — infinite but unseen. With her, he became the universe itself, reflected in every star, every soul, every breath.

This is why the universe is said to have begun with sound — the sacred syllable **AUM** — the vibration of Shakti awakening within the consciousness of Shiva.

This wasn't a conflict or a split. It was **completion**. Just as light needs shadow to be seen, creation needs both stillness and movement. This became the blueprint of all relationships — the interplay of presence and expression.

Even today, in human connections, whether romantic or spiritual, harmony arises when one partner holds space (Shiva) while the other flows with emotional expression (Shakti). This balance creates intimacy, trust, and spiritual growth.

Why This Matters to You

Most of us today are living far from cosmic harmony. The mind is noisy, restless, and overstimulated — constantly pulled by screens, deadlines, and the weight of responsibilities. Yet beneath all this activity, the soul is starving for calm. You may feel it yourself: that quiet ache inside, the longing for peace, clarity, and meaning.

Perhaps you wake up already tired, carrying the heaviness of yesterday into today. Perhaps you feel torn between wanting to achieve and wanting to rest, between craving connection and fearing vulnerability. Or maybe you've noticed how easily emotions swing — joy one moment, emptiness the next. These contradictions are not flaws in you; they are signs that the inner dance of duality has been forgotten.

Shiva–Shakti energy matters because it reminds you that these opposites are not enemies. Your stillness and your movement, your strength and your softness, your silence and your expression — all are sacred. When one side is ignored, imbalance takes root. Stress, confusion, and emotional numbness grow. But when both are honoured, something shifts: calmness returns to the mind, creativity awakens in the heart, and healing begins in the soul.

This wisdom is not abstract philosophy. It is a mirror for your daily life. It teaches you how to breathe through chaos, how to find strength in surrender, and how to transform wounds into growth. In a world that constantly pulls you outward, Shiva–Shakti calls you inward — back to the sacred union that has always lived within you.

And here is the most important truth: you are not broken; you are not incomplete. You are the union. The balance you seek is already inside you, waiting to be remembered.

The Emotional Resonance of Duality

Before you understand the universe, you must understand yourself. The same Shiva–Shakti interplay exists **within you**.

When your **inner Shiva is weak**, your thoughts scatter, your emotions control you, and you feel directionless. You become reactive instead of conscious.

When your **inner Shakti is ungrounded**, your energy becomes chaotic. You may feel anxious, overwhelmed, or intensely emotional without clarity.

This imbalance is why modern life feels exhausting.

Think of those moments when your mind is racing — overthinking conversations, worrying about the future, judging yourself harshly. This is Shakti (energy) without Shiva (stillness). You're full of movement but lacking direction.

Now think of times when you feel stuck, unmotivated, or numb — when life feels dull and repetitive. This is Shiva without Shakti. You have stillness but no spark.

Humans suffer not because life is hard, but because their inner masculine and feminine are not dancing in harmony together.

The Healing Begins with Awareness

Healing does not begin with fixing yourself; it begins with noticing yourself. Most of us are taught to either fight our emotions or bury them, but both paths leave us exhausted and disconnected. The truth is simpler, gentler: awareness is the doorway to healing.

Learning to witness your emotions like Shiva means not being controlled by them. Imagine sitting in the stillness of a mountain — storms may pass across the sky, but the mountain remains steady. In the same way, when anger, sadness, or fear arise, you can watch them without being swept away. This is Shiva's gift: the calm presence that allows you to see clearly.

Allowing yourself to feel and express emotions like Shakti means not suppressing your energy. Shakti is the river that must flow. When you give yourself permission to cry, to laugh, to dance, or to speak your truth, you honour the movement of life within you. This is Shakti's gift: the freedom to let energy move so it does not stagnate or turn into pain.

Mindfulness is simply this: Witness like Shiva. Move like Shakti. You are both the stillness and the dance. When you embrace both, you stop resisting yourself. You begin to see that your emotions are not enemies but messengers, guiding you toward balance and wholeness.

Awareness is not about perfection. It is about compassion — the willingness to sit with yourself exactly as you are. In that gentle space, healing begins. You realize that every breath carries both Shiva's stillness and Shakti's movement, and that you are already the union you seek.

Why Shakti Leads Creation

Nothing in life moves without energy. Even science reminds us that energy is the fundamental force behind all matter. Spiritually, this energy is Shakti — the pulse that awakens, the spark that ignites, the flow that carries us forward.

Shakti is the desire that awakens consciousness. She is the whisper that says, *"There is more to life than this."* She is the fuel behind intuition and creativity, the sudden inspiration that lights up your mind, the courage that pushes you to take a step into the unknown. Shakti is the spark behind transformation and manifestation — the power that turns vision into reality, thought into action, and longing into growth.

Shiva provides the space, the stillness, the awareness. He is the vast sky, the silent witness, the lamp itself. But without Shakti, there is no flame. Without her, the lamp cannot serve its purpose. It is Shakti who brings direction, intention, and movement. She is the fire that illuminates, the dance that fills the silence, the heartbeat that makes awareness come alive.

Think of your own life: every time you've felt a surge of passion, every time creativity has flowed through you, every time love or longing has moved you to act — that was Shakti. And every time you've paused, reflected, or found clarity in stillness — that was Shiva. Together, they are not separate forces but two halves of the same truth. Yet it is Shakti who always arrives first, because without energy, nothing begins. Shakti who awakens the journey — the flame that calls the lamp into purpose.

The Power and Ferocity of Shakti

People often misunderstand Shakti's fierceness. They see her intensity and mistake it for cruelty, but in truth, her power is pure strength. Shakti's ferocity is never reckless; it is purposeful. She destroys only to protect, transforms only to elevate, and becomes fierce only when necessary. Her fire is not meant to harm — it is meant to awaken.

Her ferocity teaches us valuable lessons for our own lives:

To stand up for dharma (truth): Shakti reminds us that silence in the face of injustice is not peace. Her strength calls us to rise, to defend what is right, and to live with integrity.

To release what harms us: Just as Shakti cuts away illusions, she teaches us to let go of toxic relationships, limiting beliefs, and habits that drain our energy. Her fierce love is the courage to say, *"No more."*

To break patterns of ego and attachment: Shakti's intensity burns away the false identities we cling to. She shows us that freedom comes when we release the grip of pride, fear, and attachment.

Shakti's **Ugra** (intense) form is the fire that removes darkness so the soul can shine. Imagine the way a flame clears away shadows — her energy works the same way within us. She is the force that clears confusion, dissolves stagnation, and ignites transformation. Without her, we remain stuck in cycles of fear and illusion. With her, we step into clarity, strength, and light.

CHAPTER 2

(BEYOND EGO: HOW CALMNESS AWAKENS SHAKTI)

Why Men Must Cultivate Calmness and Surrender the Ego

Modern society teaches men to be dominant, aggressive, and emotionally shut down. Yet, from the perspective of the Shiva–Shakti principle, true masculine power does not lie in control but in calmness. Calmness is not passivity—it is the steady presence that anchors both the man and his relationship.

When a man cultivates a calm mind, his masculine energy rises to its highest expression. In that calmness, he becomes a source of **stability** — the kind of presence that reassures his partner in moments of uncertainty. His steadiness is not rigid, but grounding, like the roots of a tree that hold firm even when storms pass overhead.

From this calm arises **presence** — the ability to truly see and value his partner. Presence is not about words or grand gestures; it is about being fully there, attentive and open, so she feels cherished and understood.

Protection flows naturally from this state, but it is not protection born of force or dominance. It is **protection through grounded awareness** — the quiet strength that creates safety, the assurance that she can rest in his steadiness without fear.

Calmness also awakens **wisdom**. Decisions are guided not by impulse or ego, but by clarity. He becomes someone who can discern what truly matters, leading with insight rather than reaction.

And at the heart of it all is **integrity**. Integrity builds trust, deepens intimacy, and creates a bond that cannot be shaken. It is the promise that his words and actions align, that his love is steady, and that his presence is reliable.

The greatest obstacle to this state is the **ego**. Ego thrives on proving, competing, and defending. It blocks intuition, disrupts harmony, and weakens spiritual insight. In relationships, ego manifests as the need to "win" arguments, to dominate conversations, or to resist vulnerability.

But when a man surrenders the ego, something profound happens: he opens himself to Shakti—the divine feminine energy. Shakti does not diminish him; she awakens him. She strengthens his purpose, expands his awareness, and invites him into deeper connection.

💡 Example in Relationships:

Imagine a couple facing conflict. The woman expresses her hurt, but the man's ego urges him to defend himself: "You're overreacting," or "I didn't do anything wrong." This response escalates tension and creates distance.

Now imagine the same situation with calmness. Instead of reacting, the man breathes, listens, and says, "I hear your pain. Let's understand this together." His calm presence dissolves defensiveness, allowing Shakti to flow. The woman feels safe to open her heart, and the relationship transforms from confrontation into communion.

This is the essence of Shiva–Shakti union: when masculine calmness meets feminine energy, the relationship becomes a sacred dance of balance, growth, and awakening.

Mindfulness Practice

Sit with your breath for two minutes. Place your hand on your chest and say:

"I release control. I welcome Shakti's presence within me."

Feel the warmth. This is how masculine energy softens and evolves.

Why Shiva Is Nothing Without Shakti

This truth lies at the heart of Tantra: **Shiva without Shakti is shava — a lifeless corpse.**

Shiva embodies pure consciousness—silent, vast, and eternal. But consciousness alone cannot move, create, or transform. Without Shakti, it remains potential waiting to be awakened.

Without Shakti, there is no creation.

Without Shakti, there is no movement.

Without Shakti, there is no manifestation.

Without Shakti, there is no transformation.

Shiva becomes passive, still, and unexpressed. He is the lamp without a flame, the ocean without waves, the seed without soil. Shakti is the breath that animates him, the fire that gives direction, the river that brings colour and flow to his stillness. She is the energy that turns possibility into reality, the pulse that makes consciousness alive.

A Story of Shiva Without Shakti

A famous story from Hindu mythology illustrates the importance of this relationship. One day, Parvati, the embodiment of Shakti, left Mount Kailash to visit her family. Shiva, in his meditative stillness, did not even notice her absence. He was lost in his own consciousness. But as time passed, the universe began to fall into disorder — creation itself began to falter. Shakti, in her absence, was not there to channel the divine energy that sustains life. The balance of the cosmos was at risk.

This story shows that Shakti is the energy that moves Shiva's consciousness into action. Without Shakti, there is no creation, no manifestation, no life. Even Shiva needs her energy to remain active and effective in the world.

Personal Reflection

Many people today feel spiritually unfulfilled, disconnected from their purpose. They may be highly intellectual, deeply reflective (the essence of Shiva), but without engaging with Shakti — the active, dynamic force — they feel stagnant. You may have the desire to create, to achieve, or to transform, but if you don't take action, if you don't channel your energy in the right direction, your dreams will remain mere potential.

Think of a man with great wisdom but no action. His ideas remain locked inside, never touching the world. That is Shiva without Shakti. Now imagine a woman with boundless energy but no grounding—her creativity scatters without focus. That is Shakti without Shiva.

Together, they form balance: Shiva provides the container, the steady ground. Shakti fills it with life, passion, and movement. Their union births harmony, love, and transformation.

A couple may love deeply, but if the man clings only to silence and detachment (Shiva without Shakti), the relationship feels cold and distant. When he allows Shakti—her energy, emotion, and creativity—to flow into his presence, love becomes vibrant. His calmness gives her freedom; her vitality awakens his depth.

This is why Tantra teaches that Shiva is nothing without Shakti. Consciousness needs energy to manifest. Energy needs consciousness to find direction. Only together do they create the sacred dance of life.

Mindfulness Exercise - The Awakening of Shakti:

To align yourself with this energy, try the following practice:

- Sit quietly, close your eyes, and take a few deep breaths.
- Visualize a glowing red light at the base of your spine (the root chakra).
- Imagine that light slowly rising, moving through your body with every breath.
- As the light rises, feel your energy becoming more vibrant, more alive. This is the energy of Shakti awakening within you.

Feel the flow of energy as it aligns with your consciousness (Shiva). Notice how your body begins to tingle, how your thoughts become sharper and clearer. When Shakti flows through you, the world comes alive.

CHAPTER 3

(ENERGY IS NOT GENDER: THE DIVINE FEMININE AND MASCULINE WITHIN)

The Divine Feminine and Divine Masculine

The universe is built upon the delicate balance of two energies: the Divine Feminine (Shakti) and the Divine Masculine (Shiva). Neither is superior to the other; both are essential to creation. Just as day needs night and inhale needs exhale, these energies exist in harmony, each completing the other. It is important to remember that these energies are not tied to gender. Every person carries both within them.

The Divine Feminine is the nurturing, creative, emotional, and intuitive force. She is fluid and adaptable, often associated with the earth, nature, and the cycles of life. You feel her presence in moments of compassion, in the spark of creativity, in the rhythm of your emotions, and in the quiet voice of intuition that guides you from within.

The Divine Masculine, on the other hand, is stability, consciousness, structure, and direction. He is the protector, the provider, and the conscious witness to all that exists. You experience his energy in the clarity of your decisions, in the strength that holds you steady during challenges, and in the awareness that helps you see life with perspective.

Together, these energies form the foundation of balance. The Feminine brings flow, while the Masculine brings form. The Feminine inspires, while the Masculine grounds. The Feminine creates, while the Masculine sustains. When both are honoured within us, we move through life with wholeness — able to feel deeply and act wisely, to nurture and to protect, to dream and to build.

A Story of Divine Balance: Krishna and Radha

The relationship between **Krishna** (an incarnation of Shiva) and **Radha** (the embodiment of Shakti) is a beautiful example of the balance between the masculine and feminine energies. Krishna, as the divine flute player, represents the stillness of consciousness (Shiva), while Radha, as his beloved, embodies the dynamic, passionate energy of love (Shakti).

Together, they create a perfect union of stillness and movement, of consciousness and energy. Their love is not one of attachment, but of **total surrender** — a surrender where both energies recognize their interdependence and are in harmony with the universe.

The Interplay of Shakti and Shiva

The universe exists in the interplay of these energies. Just as a river needs a riverbed, music needs silence, or a tree needs the earth, **Shakti needs Shiva to create form, and Shiva needs Shakti to bring creation to life**.

In relationships, this balance is vital. When the Divine Feminine is expressed without the structure of the Divine Masculine, it can feel chaotic, erratic, and without direction. When the Divine Masculine is expressed without the flow of the Divine Feminine, it can feel rigid, controlling, and disconnected from the heart.

This balance creates a harmonious flow, where each energy nurtures the other.

Not every relationship follows traditional energy patterns. Sometimes the woman embodies the stillness (Shiva-energy), and the man radiates the emotional force (Shakti-energy). This reversal is not dysfunction — it is diversity.

A modern example of Role Reversal

Priya and Aditya were not the "typical" couple people expected them to be. Priya was calm, steady, and deeply grounded. She rarely raised her voice, and when challenges came, she met them with quiet strength. Friends often described her as "the rock" of the relationship—embodying the stillness of **Shiva-energy**.

Aditya, on the other hand, was expressive, emotional, and full of creative fire. He cried during movies, poured his heart into music, and often spoke passionately about his dreams. His energy was vibrant, flowing, and alive—radiating the qualities of **Shakti-energy**.

At first, their families struggled to understand. "Shouldn't the man be the strong, silent one?" relatives whispered. "Isn't the woman supposed to be more emotional?" These questions carried the weight of tradition, but Priya and Aditya knew their truth.

Instead of resisting, they embraced their unique dynamic. Priya's calm presence gave Aditya the safety to express himself fully. Aditya's emotional energy brought colour and creativity into Priya's life. Together, they balanced each other beautifully.

Of course, there were challenges. Aditya sometimes felt insecure about being "too sensitive," and Priya occasionally wondered if she was "too detached." But the more they honoured their energies, the more they realized that reversal was not dysfunction—it was diversity. Their love was proof that the Divine Feminine and Masculine are not fixed roles, but living forces that flow through us in unique ways.

The truth is **Energy is not gender. Energy is blueprint.** The cure is **conscious acceptance**. When both partners understand their natural energies, harmony becomes effortless.

Why Reversals Happen

These reversals are not mistakes — they are part of the soul's journey, and they often carry lessons we are meant to learn.

Childhood conditioning: The way we were raised shapes how we express energy. If you grew up in an environment where emotions were suppressed, you may lean more into Shiva's stillness, even if your natural essence is Shakti's flow. If you were encouraged to be loud and active, you may overexpress Shakti while struggling to access Shiva's calm.

Karmic patterns: Past-life lessons can influence present dynamics. Sometimes, the soul carries unfinished experiences, and reversal happens as a way to balance what was left incomplete.

Soul contracts: Certain relationships are designed to teach balance through reversal. You may find yourself embodying more Shakti in one relationship and more Shiva in another, depending on what your soul and your partner's soul agreed to learn together.

Life experiences: Trauma, growth, or even career paths can shift energy expression. A demanding job may push you into Shiva's structure, while healing from heartbreak may awaken Shakti's emotional depth.

Natural temperament: Some people are simply born more expressive or more grounded. Reversal doesn't mean something is wrong; it means your soul is showing you another side of yourself.

⚖ Challenges in Reversed Dynamics

While reversed roles can be beautiful and even necessary for balance, they often bring distinct challenges that touch the heart in very real ways. Many readers may recognize these struggles in their own lives.

One such challenge is **misunderstanding from family**, who expect traditional patterns of masculine and feminine energy.

When your expression doesn't fit the Mold, loved ones may question or criticize, leaving you feeling unseen or unsupported.

There can also be **shame or insecurity** that arises when you feel "different" from societal norms. The world often tells us how men and women *should* behave, and when your energy flows in a way that doesn't match those expectations, it can create doubt about your worth or identity.

Another challenge is **confusion about roles** when cultural expectations clash with spiritual truth. You may feel torn between living authentically and meeting external demands, unsure of how to reconcile the two.

If the reversal is not acknowledged or embraced, it can lead to **emotional imbalance**. Suppressing your natural flow of energy — whether it is Shiva's calm or Shakti's vitality — can leave you feeling restless, disconnected, or even resentful.

Mini Practice: Identify your dominant energy

We all carry both Shiva (consciousness) and Shakti (energy) within us. The key is noticing which one flows more naturally in your everyday life. This isn't about gender—it's about energy.

Take a quiet moment and ask yourself:

- Am I naturally more emotional or calm?
  - ✓ Do I feel things deeply and express them, or do I hold steady and grounded?
- Do I lead with intuition or logic?

  - ✓ Do I trust my gut feelings, or do I prefer analysing and planning?
- Do I crave movement or stillness?
  - ✓ Do I thrive in action and change, or do I feel at home in silence and stability?

This practice is about self-awareness. When you know your dominant energy, you can honour it instead of fighting it—while also learning to invite the opposite energy when you need balance. That's where growth and harmony begin.

PART 2

CHAPTER 4

(TWIN FLAMES — THE SACRED MIRROR OF SHIVA AND SHAKTI)

The Concept of Twin Flames

The concept of twin flames arises from the understanding that two souls can originate from the same source, carrying within them the living reflection of Shiva and Shakti in human form. This connection is not confined to romance, though it often gets mistaken for it. Twin flames may appear as lovers, as well as friends, mentors, or even challengers. What defines them is not the role they play but the intensity of recognition — a magnetic pull that feels both exhilarating and unsettling, as though one has met a mirror of their own soul.

The purpose of this union is far higher than personal fulfilment. Twin flames come together to awaken each other, to stir dormant energies, and to challenge the shadows that lie hidden within. They trigger growth by reflecting back the parts of ourselves we would rather avoid, dissolving layers of ego that keep us bound to illusion. In this way, the twin flame journey becomes a crucible of transformation, refining and expanding the soul.

Each twin flame carries a polarity of the divine energies. One may embody more of Shiva — stillness, awareness, detachment, the silent witness. The other may embody more of Shakti — movement, emotion, creativity, the vibrant force of life. Their union is not about dominance or hierarchy but about balance. Together, they reveal surrender, acceptance, and unconditional love. Just as Shiva without Shakti is pure consciousness without expression, and Shakti without Shiva is energy without direction, so too do twin flames remind us that wholeness is found only when both aspects are embraced.

The journey of twin flames often unfolds in stages. At first there is recognition — a sudden, undeniable sense of familiarity, as if two souls have known each other across lifetimes. This recognition is followed by challenge, where the intensity of the bond brings hidden wounds to the surface. Often, this leads to separation, a period of distance that feels painful but is necessary for inner work and healing. In time, as both individuals grow into greater authenticity, alignment occurs. Ego dissolves, and the connection shifts from turbulence to harmony. Union, then, is not always physical but spiritual — a merging of energies where balance and unconditional love are realized.

Ultimately, the twin flame connection is not meant to serve the self alone. Its purpose is collective. When twin flames embody the sacred mirror of Shiva and Shakti, their union radiates outward, inspiring others to awaken. Their alignment becomes a force of healing, a ripple of transformation that touches the world. Just as Shiva and Shakti together create the cosmos, twin flames together create a field of consciousness that invites others into remembrance of their own divine nature.

💞 Emotional Depth

Meeting a twin flame often feels overwhelming because it stirs the deepest layers of the soul. It is as though a hidden door suddenly opens, releasing currents of energy that touch places within you that you may not have known existed. Old wounds rise to the surface, demanding acknowledgment. Hidden fears that have long been buried begin to speak. Deep desires, some radiant and some shadowed, awaken with intensity. Even spiritual memories — echoes of lifetimes past — may resurface, carrying with them a sense of déjà vu that is both haunting and comforting.

This intensity is not chaos, though it may feel like it. It is transformation. The twin flame connection shakes you awake, refusing to let you remain in the comfort of avoidance. It forces you to confront what you have hidden, what you have denied, and what you have resisted. In doing so, it invites you into profound healing. The turbulence is not punishment but purification, a sacred fire that burns away illusions and reveals the truth of who you are.

This emotional depth is unlike any other journey. It is raw, unfiltered, and often disorienting. Yet within the overwhelm lies the gift: the chance to dissolve layers of ego and step into greater authenticity. The twin flame becomes both mirror and catalyst, reflecting your inner landscape with uncompromising clarity and igniting the courage to transform.

To walk this path is to surrender to love in its most demanding form — a love that does not flatter or soothe, but insists on growth. It is the love of Shiva and Shakti themselves, a love that dismantles and rebuilds, that destroys illusion and creates truth. Emotional depth in the twin flame journey is not simply about feeling more; it is about being reshaped by the very force of divine polarity, until you emerge more whole, more awake, and more aligned with your soul's purpose.

The Twin Flame Journey

The journey of twin flames is rarely smooth. It is a path marked by intensity, challenge, and profound transformation. To meet your twin flame is to encounter both ecstasy and agony in the same breath. Their presence awakens a joy so expansive it feels like coming home, yet it also stirs the deepest wounds you carry. They reflect back not only your highest potential but also the shadows you have long tried to escape.

This reflection is not meant to break you, but to liberate you. In their gaze, you cannot hide from yourself. Old patterns rise to the surface, demanding release. Unresolved pain insists on healing. The twin flame connection becomes a sacred fire, burning away illusions and forcing you to grow spiritually. It is a journey that insists on authenticity, stripping away masks until only the truth of your soul remains.

At times, this path feels unbearable. The intensity of the bond can lead to separation, as both flames retreat to process the overwhelming emotions it stirs. Yet even in distance, the connection continues to work within you, reshaping your inner world. The longing, the triggers, the magnetic pull — all of it serves a higher purpose: to bring you closer to unity, not only with another person but with the divine energies within yourself.

When both flames surrender to this process, harmony begins to emerge. The turbulence softens into balance, and the connection shifts from chaos to sacred rhythm. In this state, the twin flames embody the perfect balance of Shiva and Shakti — the masculine and feminine energies dancing together in union. Shiva's stillness and Shakti's movement no longer clash but complement, creating a wholeness that radiates outward.

Ultimately, the twin flame journey is not about possession or permanence. It is about awakening. It teaches that love in its truest form is not bound by ego or fear, but flows freely as a force of transformation. To walk this path is to discover that the union of twin flames is not simply between two souls, but between the fragmented and the whole, the human and the divine, the self and the cosmos.

The Mirror of the Soul – The Cosmic Reflection

Meeting your twin flame is like gazing into the clearest mirror you have ever known. In their presence, you cannot hide. You see your own shadows, your light, your fears, and your deepest desires reflected back to you with startling clarity. This reflection is not always comfortable; in fact, it can be profoundly unsettling. Yet it is precisely this discomfort that becomes the doorway to growth. The twin flame does not arrive to flatter or soothe — they arrive to awaken.

Through the mirror of the twin flame, you are invited into a process of deep healing and transformation. Every wound that has been buried, every fear that has been silenced, every longing that has been denied begins to surface. Their energy acts as a catalyst, stirring the soul into remembrance of its divine origin. What emerges is not chaos but alchemy: the raw material of your human experience being transmuted into wisdom, compassion, and a deeper connection to the divine energy within.

It is important to understand that twin flames are not a romantic plotline with guaranteed bliss. They are not the fairy tale of effortless love. Instead, they are shock therapy for the soul — a jolt of truth that dismantles illusions and demands authenticity. Two halves of one original energy cut across lifetimes to meet, mirror, and catalyse each other. Their union is not about comfort but about awakening, not about permanence but about transformation.

The intensity of this meeting can be both ecstatic and excruciating. Ecstasy arises when you glimpse your highest capacities reflected back — the brilliance of your soul, the boundless love you are capable of embodying. Excruciation comes when the deepest unresolved material is triggered — the pain, the fear, the attachments that must be released. In this way, the twin flame journey becomes a cosmic reflection, a sacred mirror that reveals the totality of who you are.

To walk this path is to embrace the paradox: that the same person who brings you to your knees in agony is also the one who lifts you into the heights of ecstasy. The mirror of the soul does not lie. It shows you everything — the divine and the human, the broken and the whole. And in that reflection, you are given the chance to remember that you are both Shiva and Shakti, consciousness and energy, stillness and movement. The twin flame connection is the cosmic reminder that within you lies the capacity for union, balance, and unconditional love.

🎇 When to engage and when to step back

Not every twin flame connection is meant to last forever. The meeting of twin flames is always purposeful, but the form it takes may not always be sustainable. Sometimes the intensity of the bond can illuminate the path forward; at other times, it can reveal wounds so raw that remaining together becomes destructive. When a relationship is marked by repeated abuse, addiction, or harm, stepping away is not abandonment but the truest honouring of both souls. To disengage in such moments is to recognize that love cannot flourish where suffering is normalized.

The twin flame journey is not a mandate to endure pain for the sake of growth. Growth does not require self-sacrifice in the form of harm. In fact, one of the deepest lessons twin flames teach is discernment — the ability to know when engagement fosters healing and when distance protects the integrity of the soul. Healthy boundaries are not a rejection of the connection; they are a spiritual practice in themselves. To say "no" when love becomes distorted is to affirm the sanctity of both Shiva and Shakti within you.

Engaging with a twin flame can be transformative when the connection inspires authenticity, courage, and healing. It can feel like a sacred dance where both partners rise together, each reflecting the other's highest potential. But when the dance turns into a cycle of harm, stepping back becomes the act of wisdom. Just as Shiva embodies detachment and Shakti embodies flow, sometimes the balance requires stillness, distance, and space for each soul to heal independently.

Ultimately, the twin flame journey is about unity with the divine energies within yourself. Whether you remain close to your twin flame or choose to walk away, the purpose is the same: to awaken to your own wholeness. To engage is sacred, but so too is the courage to step back. Both are acts of love, both are acts of truth, and both honour the cosmic mirror that twin flames reveal.

🌿 A short practice: Cleansing mirror ritual (10 minutes)

This practice is designed to help you recognize the lessons your relationships mirror back to you and to invite healing through self-awareness. It is simple, yet deeply transformative.

- **Prepare the space**
  - ✓ Sit before a mirror with a candle lit nearby. Allow the flame to symbolize illumination and clarity
- **Meet your reflection**
  - ✓ Breathe deeply and say aloud, “I see you. I own my shadow. I choose healing.”
- **Identify patterns**
  - ✓ Write down three patterns you believe the other awakens in you. Next to each, write one small action you can take to heal it.
- **Seal the rituals**
  - ✓ Place your hand over your heart, bow slightly to your reflection, and feel gratitude for the mirror of the soul. Close with a moment of silence, honouring both your Shiva (consciousness) and Shakti (energy).

This ritual is not about judgment—it is about cleansing. By owning your shadow and choosing healing, you transform the intensity of the twin flame mirror into a path of growth, balance, and love.

CHAPTER 5

(MANIFESTATION THROUGH BALANCED ENERGIES)

Manifestation is not about wishful thinking or simply desiring something until it appears. It is the sacred union of Shiva and Shakti within you — the balance of clarity and energy, vision and movement. Shiva represents clarity. He is the silent architect, the blueprint of intention, the stillness that asks: *What do I truly want?* His presence is the mind's focus, the awareness that shapes vision with precision and purpose.

Shakti, on the other hand, is movement. She is the passion, the creative force that breathes life into vision. Shakti asks: *How do I bring this into reality?* Her energy is the heartbeat of manifestation, the flow that transforms ideas into tangible form. Where Shiva designs, Shakti animates. Where Shiva holds the vision, Shakti carries it into the world with vitality and devotion.

When Shiva — the mind — is focused, and Shakti — the heart — is aligned, manifestation flows naturally. It is not forced, nor is it chaotic. It becomes a dance of balance, where clarity guides energy and energy fulfils clarity. This union teaches us that manifestation is not about chasing desires blindly, but about harmonizing thought and feeling, intention and action.

To manifest through balanced energies is to embody Shiva's stillness and Shakti's dynamism together. It is to hold a clear vision while allowing the creative force to move freely, trusting that the cosmos responds when inner balance is achieved. In this way, manifestation becomes less about control and more about surrender — surrender to the sacred rhythm of consciousness and energy working together.

ॐ Shiva's Role in Manifestation:

Shiva is the stillness that defines purpose. He is the silent centre, the unshakable presence that holds the seed of creation before it takes form. Without Shiva, energy scatters in countless directions, unfocused and restless. It is his stillness that gathers the currents of possibility into a single point of clarity. Shiva gives intention, the pure awareness that asks what is truly desired. He gives vision, the blueprint that shapes the path ahead. And he gives direction, the guiding force that ensures energy does not wander aimlessly but flows toward fulfilment.

In manifestation, Shiva is the clarity that guides Shakti's flow. He is the architect of consciousness, the one who sketches the design before Shakti breathes life into it. His role is not action but awareness, not movement but definition. When Shiva's presence is strong within you, your desires are no longer vague impulses; they become purposeful intentions. His stillness teaches that manifestation begins not with doing, but with knowing

— knowing what you seek, why it matters, and how it aligns with your soul's truth.

Shakti's Role in Manifestation:

Shakti is the fire that moves creation. She is the living pulse, the energy that transforms vision into reality. Without her, clarity remains only thought, a silent blueprint that never breathes. It is Shakti who brings emotion, stirring the heart with feeling and resonance. It is Shakti who awakens passion, igniting the desire to act and to create. And it is Shakti who carries action forward, turning intention into movement, dream into form.

She is the heartbeat of manifestation, the rhythm that animates the stillness of Shiva's design. Where Shiva defines purpose, Shakti gives it life. She flows through every step of creation, reminding us that manifestation is not only about knowing what we want but about embodying the energy that brings it forth. In her dance, clarity becomes creation, and vision becomes reality.

Dancing Energies - A Practice of Creation:

The first step belongs to Shiva, the silent architect of creation. To embody his presence, sit in stillness and allow the mind to quiet. In that silence, ask yourself: What do I truly desire? Why do I want it? How will it serve my highest self? Shiva's energy is clarity — he defines the vision, stripping away distractions until only the essence of your intention remains.

Shakti fuels the vision with emotion, passion, and vitality. To embody her, feel your desire as though it already exists. Let joy, gratitude, excitement, and love flow through you, filling every cell of your being. In this state, you are not simply imagining; you are embodying the vibration of what you seek, allowing Shakti's energy to carry it into the universe.

Shiva holds the vision. Shakti moves the universe. Together, they manifest. This is the cosmic rhythm: stillness guiding movement, movement fulfilling stillness.

💡 From Vision to Reality - Illustration:

Kiran's Business Dream -

Consider Kiran's journey with his business dream. For years, he carried ideas within him — the clarity of Shiva was present, but the movement of Shakti was missing. His visions remained sketches in the mind, never stepping into reality. After committing to meditation, something shifted. Stillness brought him deeper clarity, and from that clarity arose emotion — excitement, gratitude, and a renewed sense of purpose. With Shakti awakened, he began taking small, consistent steps each day. Within months, opportunities began to appear. They did not arrive by chance, but through alignment. His inner balance of Shiva and Shakti created the outer flow that carried his dream forward.

Dev's Relationship Journey

Dev's story unfolded in a different way, yet it reveals the same truth. He longed for love, but beneath that longing was a belief that he was "not enough." His desire was strong, but his energy was weak, weighed down by self-doubt. The imbalance kept love at a distance. Through healing practices, Dev shifted his vibration. He released the old belief and allowed Shakti's energy to rise within him. As his heart opened, he became magnetic. Love did not require effort or pursuit; it found him naturally; drawn to the harmony he had cultivated within.

Both Kiran and Dev show us that manifestation is not about forcing outcomes. It is about balance. When Shiva's clarity defines the vision and Shakti's energy fuels the movement, life responds. Opportunities, relationships, and experiences flow not as accidents, but as reflections of the inner dance of consciousness and energy.

🤔 Why Manifestation Fails:

Manifestation often falters because wanting and being aligned are not the same. Desire alone cannot call something into existence if the energy behind it is fragmented or contradictory. You cannot manifest love while rooted in insecurity, because the vibration of fear repels the very intimacy you seek. You cannot manifest abundance while clinging to scarcity, because the belief in lack blocks the flow of prosperity. You cannot manifest peace while living in chaos, because the restless energy continues to recreate turmoil. And you cannot manifest clarity while operating from fear, because fear clouds vision and distorts truth.

The essence of manifestation lies in resonance. Your energy must match your desire. When the inner state contradicts the outer intention, the universe responds not to the words you speak but to the vibration you carry. This is why so many attempts at manifestation feel frustrating — the mind may declare a wish, but the heart and energy remain misaligned.

True manifestation requires harmony between thought, feeling, and action. It is not enough to want; you must become. To manifest love, you must embody self-worth and openness. To manifest abundance, you must cultivate trust in flow and generosity. To manifest peace, you must nurture stillness within. To manifest clarity, you must release fear and embrace truth. When your inner state reflects the reality you seek, manifestation becomes natural, effortless, and inevitable.

🌿 Extra Practices:

- **Daily Check-In:** Write one clear intention (Shiva) and one emotion you embodied (Shakti).
  - ✓ You can use manifestation techniques like **369** (write your intention 3 times in the morning, 6 times midday, 9 times at night) or **555** (write your desire 55 times for 5 days).
  - ✓ This repetition imprints clarity and emotion into your subconscious, aligning thought and energy.
- **Embodiment Ritual:** Dance for 5 minutes (Shakti), then sit in silence for 5 minutes (Shiva).
  - ✓ While moving, visualize energy flowing through you like water
  - ✓ While sitting, focus on your breath—inhale to invite Shakti, exhale to ground into Shiva.
- **Gratitude Alignment:** Before bed, write three gratitude (Shakti) and one vision for tomorrow (Shiva).
  - ✓ Add the **Ho'oponopono practice** by softly repeating:

"I'm sorry. Please forgive me. Thank you. I love you."

✓ Before bed, write down **three gratitude** (Shakti) and **one vision for tomorrow** (Shiva).

- **Visualization with Elements:**
  ✓ Hold a glass of water, speak your intention into it (Shiva), then drink it while feeling gratitude (Shakti).
  ✓ Inhale clarity (Shiva), exhale energy (Shakti). Repeat for 9 breaths.

Manifestation is not magic—it is **energetic precision**. When Shiva and Shakti unite, creation becomes effortless. It is not about forcing reality, but becoming the version of yourself who naturally receives it.

CHAPTER 6

(EMOTIONAL WOUNDS AND ENERGY IMBALANCE)

Every soul carries scars — unspoken fears, memories that still ache, and disappointments that never found closure. These wounds do not simply disappear with the passing of time. Instead, they linger quietly, shaping the way we feel and respond to life. They may surface as anxiety that unsettles the mind, anger that erupts unexpectedly, loneliness that weighs on the heart, or self-doubt that clouds our sense of worth.

Healing is not about erasing the past or pretending that pain never existed. It is about restoring balance to the energies that were disrupted during those painful experiences. When a wound remains unhealed, it distorts the natural flow of energy within us. Shiva's clarity becomes clouded, and Shakti's movement loses rhythm. The imbalance can make us feel stuck, unable to move forward, or trapped in cycles that repeat the same lessons over and over.

Healing begins by bringing awareness to these scars, acknowledging them without judgment, and allowing their stored energy to be released and transformed. It is not about denying the story of our pain but about rewriting its influence. When balance is restored, the same experiences that once felt heavy become sources of wisdom and strength. The soul learns to carry its past not as a burden but as a teacher, guiding it toward greater wholeness.

Emotional wounds remind us that manifestation and growth cannot flourish in fractured energy. Only when we tend to the places within us that ache can we invite harmony back into our being. Healing, then, is the art of returning to balance — of allowing Shiva's stillness and Shakti's vitality to once again dance together, so that the soul can move freely toward its highest expression.

How Emotional Wounds Disturb Shiva and Shakti

When trauma strikes, it unsettles the delicate inner balance that sustains our well-being. Shiva, the energy of consciousness and clarity, becomes weakened, leaving the mind restless, unstable, and unable to hold steady vision. Shakti, the energy of emotion and movement, grows turbulent, creating storms of insecurity, overwhelm, or emotional intensity that feel impossible to contain. When these energies fall out of harmony, they weave ego-driven stories that disconnect us from the divine flow, pulling us away from our natural state of balance.

Think of a relationship that ended abruptly. In such a moment, you may have felt torn between two extremes — the yearning for clarity that belongs to Shiva and the flood of emotions that belong to Shakti. Crying, overthinking, or feeling helpless was not weakness; it was the natural result of energies moving out of sync. The mind sought answers while the heart overflowed with pain, and the imbalance between Shiva and Shakti magnified the suffering.

Many people respond to this disruption by suppressing one energy. Some silence Shakti by refusing to feel, numbing themselves to emotion in the hope of regaining control. Others suppress Shiva by refusing to reflect, drowning in feeling without allowing clarity to guide them. Yet neither path brings true healing. Healing begins only when both energies are honoured — when Shiva's stillness is restored to bring perspective, and Shakti's movement is allowed to flow freely, releasing emotion without judgment.

Acknowledging both energies invites balance back into soul. It is to recognize that clarity without feeling becomes cold detachment, while feeling without clarity becomes chaos. True healing is the reunion of Shiva and Shakti, where consciousness steadies' emotion and emotion enlivens consciousness. In this union, the wounds of the past no longer dictate the present, and the soul can once again move in harmony with the divine rhythm of life.

Healing the Wounded Masculine and Feminine

Every person carries wounds shaped by childhood experiences, societal conditioning, and past relationships. These wounds do not simply disappear; they often take shape as distortions in our inner masculine and feminine energies — Shiva and Shakti. When these energies are wounded, they lose their natural balance and begin to express themselves in ways that keep us disconnected from our true essence.

The wounded masculine often shows up as emotional numbness, a fear of vulnerability, or a tendency to control. Instead of offering stillness, it hardens into rigidity. Instead of guiding with awareness, it collapses into avoidance. This distortion creates a shell around the heart, making it difficult to trust, to surrender, or to connect deeply with oneself and others.

The wounded feminine, on the other hand, often manifests as over-giving, emotional overwhelm, insecurity, or attachment rooted in fear of abandonment. Instead of flowing freely, her energy becomes chaotic. Instead of nurturing, her emotions spill uncontained, leaving her drained and dependent on external validation. This imbalance clouds intuition and makes it difficult to feel safe within one's own emotional landscape.

Healing begins not by fixing others or trying to change external circumstances, but by recognizing these wounds within ourselves. It is an inward journey of awareness — noticing where Shiva's clarity has hardened into avoidance, and where Shakti's flow has dissolved into chaos. By gently acknowledging these distortions, we begin to restore balance. The wounded masculine softens into true stillness, and the wounded feminine steadies into empowered flow. Together, they return to harmony, allowing us to embody both strength and sensitivity, clarity and compassion.

The Inner Child — Healing the First Wound of Shakti

At the heart of every imbalance lies the inner child — that tender part of the soul which remembers every joy, every fear, and every wound. Shakti, the emotional force within us, finds her earliest expression through this inner child. She is the raw, unfiltered energy of feeling, the innocence that laughs freely, cries openly, and loves without hesitation. Yet when childhood wounds remain unhealed, they echo through our adult struggles, shaping the way we relate to ourselves and with others.

Imagine a child who was constantly told to "stop crying." Each time their tears were silenced, they learned to believe that emotions were a weakness. Over time, this belief hardened into a pattern. As they grew older, they hid their feelings, struggled to communicate openly, avoided vulnerability, and carried a quiet sense of unworthiness in deep love. What began as a simple wound in childhood became a lifelong distortion of Shakti's flow.

It was only when they finally turned inward and acknowledged the presence of their inner child that the truth became clear. Their emotional patterns were not flaws or failures — they were unhealed wounds asking for attention. The inner child was not broken; she was waiting to be seen, heard, and embraced.

Healing the inner child is the first step toward restoring Shakti in her purest form. When we allow ourselves to feel what was once denied, Shakti awakens as playful, creative, fearless, and loving energy. She becomes the vibrant force that reconnects us to joy, to authenticity, and to the freedom of emotional expression. In this healing, the soul learns that vulnerability is not weakness but strength, and that the tender child within us is the key to reclaiming balance and wholeness.

Emotional Alchemy — Turning Pain into Wisdom

Shakti is the alchemist of emotion. She takes raw pain and, when allowed to move freely, transforms it into strength.

One man once carried heartbreak like a stone in his chest after his partner left unexpectedly. He tried distractions — work, gym, friends — but nothing soothed the ache. One night, exhausted, he stopped resisting and allowed himself to fully feel the grief. He breathed into the pain instead of tightening against it. Within minutes, something shifted: the grief softened, then moved, then released. This was emotional alchemy — pain transmuting because it was finally witnessed, not suppressed.

Pain transforms when Shiva, the witness, creates space, and Shakti, the emotion, flows and releases. Together they heal what suppression keeps alive.

A simple practice: place your hand on your chest, inhale deeply, exhale with a soft sigh, and whisper, *"I am safe to feel this."* Even a small shift is healing.

Male Calmness and the Release of Ego

True masculine strength is not loud or dominating. It is quiet, steady, and present. This is Shiva's calm — the ability to hold space without trying to fix or control.

One man, caught in cycles of anger and defensiveness, realized his rage was only a shield for fear — fear of not being enough, fear of vulnerability. He began a simple practice: pausing for thirty seconds before replying in conflict. At first it felt awkward, but slowly his reactions softened. His presence became his power. His partner began to share instead of shutting down, and intimacy returned.

When ego softens, intimacy deepens. Presence is not weakness; it is spaciousness. It allows Shakti to flow without fear, and relationships to breathe without control.

Releasing the male ego begins with cultivating presence rather than reaction. In moments of conflict, pause and silently count to five, allowing Shiva's stillness to settle the mind before words arise. Replace defensiveness with curiosity by asking, *"Tell me more,"* which opens space for Shakti's flow instead of shutting it down. Practice humility by admitting, *"I was wrong,"* when necessary, softening the rigid walls of ego and inviting compassion. In this state, masculine energy transforms — no longer driven by dominance, but rooted in presence, spaciousness, and peace.

Shakti's Ferocity and Compassion

Shakti is not a single tone. She can be soft as moonlight and sharp as lightning. Her fierce form — Ugra — is decisive, uncompromising, and purifying. That ferocity exists to defend life, uproot falsehood, and clear the way for real love to grow.

There was a woman, Meera, who had tolerated small cruelties from a partner for years: belittling comments, cancelled plans, excuses. Friends told her to be patient. Her inner voice — quiet at first — began to bloom into a steady flame. One evening, after a conversation that ended with another apology and the same pattern, Meera felt something rise in her chest. It was not rage alone; it was clarity. She said, simply, "I will not let this be my life," and she left.

Her action felt violent to some, soft to others, but inside it was Shakti's righteous clarity. She was not fleeing anger — she was defending her dignity. Over time her life reorganized: new friendships, a job that respected her, creative projects she previously shelved. The ferocity had saved her capacity to love — and opened space for tenderness that was real.

Shakti's intensity removes what is rotten. It forces truth to the surface. This is a spiritual act. The fire does not exist to punish, but to transform.

To handle Shakti's ferocity, the first step is to recognize when a boundary has been crossed. Awareness itself is empowering, because it prevents confusion and gives clarity to your response. Once you see the breach, speak with firmness but without destruction — clarity is far more powerful than chaos. After taking action, pause and centre yourself so that righteous energy does not slip into pride or aggression. Finally, let compassion follow the boundary you have set. True ferocity is not about antagonism; it is about protecting dignity while leaving space for love to return.

Integration brings balance

Healing through Shiva–Shakti balance is not about choosing one energy over the other. It is about honouring both. Shiva offers presence, silence, and steadiness. Shakti offers movement, emotion, and transformation. Together they create wholeness.

When pain arises, witness it with Shiva's calm. Allow it to move with Shakti's flow. When energy floods, act. When stillness calls, rest. When ego demands control, soften. When boundaries are crossed, let Shakti's fire speak with clarity.

Healing is not about removing pain. It is about restoring the dance.

CHAPTER 7

(RELATIONSHIPS AS SPIRITUAL MIRRORS)

Relationships are not accidents. Whether romantic, familial, or friendships, they are spiritual mirrors reflecting both our strengths and our blind spots. Through them, we discover where we are balanced and where we are wounded. The Shiva–Shakti lens teaches us that relationships thrive not on rigid roles or gender expectations, but on the balance of energies. Understanding Energy in Relationships.

The Energies at Play

In every partnership, one energy offers presence — the calm, steady awareness of Shiva. The other offers expression — the flowing, emotional movement of Shakti. At their best, these roles are not fixed; they shift and interchange, creating harmony. But when imbalance arises, friction follows.

Modern life often distorts this natural rhythm. Many women are pushed into masculine energy — drive, logic, control — while many men are disconnected from their emotional and intuitive selves. This imbalance breeds misunderstanding and emotional distance.

Imagine a woman expressing her feelings with intensity. Her partner, overwhelmed, reacts defensively, unable to hold space. Arguments erupt, silence follows, and separation looms. Yet when the man grounds himself in Shiva's calmness, he can hold her expression without fear. And when the woman allows her Shakti to move with awareness, she flows instead of overwhelms. Balance restores harmony.

Practices for Harmony

Healing relationships begins with small shifts. For men, the practice is listening without rushing to fix. For women, it is expressing emotions with clarity rather than chaos. For both, the guiding question is simple: *"Am I acting from fear or from love?"*

When Shiva and Shakti are honoured equally, relationships transform. You feel calm yet alive, take inspired rather than impulsive action, attract healthier connections, and trust the universe without forcing outcomes. Harmony brings ease.

Why Harmony Matters

Shiva offers direction, structure, focus, and stillness. Shakti brings creativity, joy, passion, and intuition. When they unite, they create purposeful passion — wisdom guided by energy, clarity fuelled by inspiration.

One man discovered this when his ambition faltered. Some days he was motivated, other days lost. Learning about Shiva–Shakti harmony changed everything. He used Shiva's clarity to set goals and Shakti's flow to stay inspired. Within months, his career grew, his confidence deepened, and his emotional life stabilized. His success was not luck — it was energetic alignment.

The Energetic Blueprint of Relationships

Every relationship is an energetic exchange. Failures are rarely about incompatibility; they stem from unbalanced energies. When one partner becomes overly emotional, the other instinctively turns logical. When one grows chaotic, the other becomes controlling. When one withdraws, the other clings. These are not flaws but compensations — attempts to restore balance.

Consider a couple who loved each other deeply yet argued constantly. She overflowed with emotion, while he withdrew into silence. Once they understood Shiva–Shakti dynamics, everything shifted. He practiced presence instead of avoidance. She grounded her emotions instead of overwhelming. Their energies balanced, and so did their relationship.

The Spiritual Lesson

People rarely hurt us intentionally. They react from their energetic wounds. When we begin to see the energy behind someone's behaviour, compassion replaces conflict. Relationships stop being battlegrounds and become classrooms — places where we learn, heal, and grow.

The Sacred Union Within

The greatest spiritual journey is not the search for a soulmate, a god, or even a grand purpose. It is the journey toward **inner**

union — the merging of Shiva's stillness and Shakti's vitality. Most people live with these forces in conflict: the mind arguing with the heart, logic suppressing emotion, desires contradicting responsibilities. This inner battle creates confusion, unstable relationships, and restlessness.

Inner union is the moment you stop fighting yourself. It is when intuition and intelligence begin working together, when calmness and passion coexist, when silence and creativity dance as one. In this state, you no longer chase validation or external completion. You finally feel whole.

A Relatable Story

Maya spent years thinking a relationship would fix her emptiness. She believed love from another person would fill the void inside her. But every time she entered a relationship, her fears, insecurities, and emotional turbulence resurfaced.

One day, during meditation, she had a realization:

She wasn't seeking a partner. She was seeking herself.

She began grounding herself through breathing (Shiva) and awakening her creativity through art (Shakti). The more she understood her energies, the more confident and secure she became.

Inner union transformed her life more than any relationship ever could.

PART 3

CHAPTER 8

(THE PATH OF SOUL GROWTH/ THE SACRED POWER OF SURRENDER)

Surrender is one of the most misunderstood yet transformative spiritual teachings. Many equate it with defeat, but in the Shiva–Shakti philosophy, surrender means trusting the divine flow. It is not about giving up; it is about opening up.

Shiva's surrender is the surrender to silence, meditation, and universal truth. It is not weakness but mastery of self. In surrender, Shiva becomes limitless, dissolving into pure consciousness.

Shakti's surrender is the surrender to movement and transformation. She does not resist change; she becomes it. Her strength lies not in control but in trust — trust in intuition, trust in the unfolding design of the universe.

For us as humans, surrender means letting go of the need to control outcomes, allowing emotions to be felt fully, trusting that the universe is working in our favour, and embracing inner flow instead of outer force.

The Bhagavad Gita offers a timeless example. On the battlefield, Arjuna was paralyzed by doubt and emotion. Krishna, embodying Shiva consciousness, did not force him but guided him through the fog of ego. Arjuna's surrender was not to defeat but to clarity — and from clarity came strength, purpose, and divine action.

The Courage to Hold Space

A simple practice can open this doorway: sit quietly, place your hand on your chest, and whisper, "I surrender my worries. I trust my path. I accept what I cannot control." Notice how the heart softens when resistance is released.

Surrender is not passive. It is active trust. When you try to control every detail of your life, you only meet resistance. But when you surrender — listening to intuition, trusting timing, and allowing life to unfold — opportunities appear effortlessly. You discover that surrender does not diminish power; it awakens a greater one.

Yet surrender is only half the dance. The other half is the courage to hold space. There are moments when movement is not the answer, when emotions need a container. That container is Shiva. To hold space means to stay grounded when others are emotional, to listen without fixing, to remain calm in chaos, and to offer stability instead of solutions.

A person once struggled with their partner's emotional storms, reacting quickly and trying to fix everything. This constant need to respond only created more conflict. Over time, they discovered the power of Shiva's stillness. Instead of defending, they began to breathe. Instead of reacting, they chose to listen. For the first time, their partner felt truly heard, and for the first time, they themselves felt peaceful. The relationship deepened because Shiva's presence was able to hold Shakti's expression, creating harmony where there had once been chaos.

The lesson is clear- Shakti heals through expression; Shiva heals through presence. Both are necessary. Both are sacred. Together, they show us that surrender is not defeat but divine alignment — the union of flow and stillness, trust and presence.

The Scared Art of Letting Go

Not all endings arrive with thunder. Some happen quietly, almost invisibly, like the slow dimming of a candle. A relationship may dissolve not through betrayal or explosive fights, but through silence. Conversations grow shorter, laughter fades, and the space between two souls becomes heavier. One evening, a partner may whisper, *"When did we stop meeting each other?"* and the only answer is tears — not of anger, but of truth.

This kind of drifting is not failure; it is transition. Emotional needs evolve, growth unfolds at different speeds, and energies fall out of rhythm. Past wounds quietly shape behaviour until two paths diverge. The lesson is not to search for villains or to assign blame, but to honour the love that was shared. Every connection, no matter how brief or how long, leaves an imprint on the soul. To let go is to acknowledge that the chapter has ended, while still holding gratitude for the story it told.

Closure does not come from forcing answers or demanding explanations. It comes from gratitude — from the gentle recognition that what was once alive and nourishing has served its purpose. A simple practice can help soften this process: write a letter you will never send, beginning with the words, *"Thank you for the moments that made me who I am."* Allow your tears to bless the memory rather than harden your heart. In this way, letting go becomes less about loss and more about release, a sacred surrender that honours both yourself and the love that once was.

Lessons from Shiva — The Power of Detachment

Detachment is often misunderstood as coldness, but in truth it is clarity. Shiva teaches us that when we release ego, fear, insecurity, and the constant need to control outcomes, we create space for real love and wisdom to enter. Detachment is not about withdrawing from life or refusing to care; it is about seeing clearly, without being bound by illusions or attachments that distort our vision.

One person once lived chained to career success, defining their worth entirely by how others perceived them. Every setback felt like collapse, every mistake like self-betrayal. Their identity was tied so tightly to achievement that failure seemed unbearable. In meditation, they remembered Shiva's image — serene in the Himalayas, unmoved by storms, resting in stillness while the world around him shifted endlessly. Suddenly, it clicked: success should be an expression of energy, not a measurement of worth. This realization freed them. They continued to work hard, but no longer as prisoners of outcome. Their efforts became offerings rather than burdens, and detachment became liberation.

Shiva's lesson is simple yet profound: when we let go of control, we discover freedom. Shakti moves, Shiva watches. One flows with passion, the other holds with presence. When both are honoured, emotional freedom is born. In this balance, we learn that surrender is not weakness but strength — the strength to trust life's rhythm, to act with devotion, and to release the need for certainty. Detachment, in Shiva's way, is the doorway to peace.

Lessons from Shakti — The Power of Expression

If Shiva teaches stillness, Shakti teaches movement. If Shiva teaches silence, Shakti teaches voice. Shakti is the heartbeat of the universe — the fire, the dance, the breath that makes existence vibrant. She is the pulse that animates creation, the energy that transforms vision into lived experience. Where Shiva offers the container, Shakti fills it with colour, rhythm, and vitality.

Suppressing emotions does not make one spiritual; it makes one disconnected. To deny Shakti is to deny life itself. Expression is not indulgence — it is healing, liberation, and authenticity. Through expression, the soul releases what has been held too tightly and opens to the flow of truth.

One person grew up believing emotions were weakness. They bottled up pain, desires, even joy, until numbness set in. Life became muted, as though the fire within had been extinguished. In a healing circle, they were introduced to Shakti — the divine feminine energy that flows freely, unapologetically. For the first time, they allowed themselves to cry in front of others. Not out of weakness, but out of truth. In that release, they felt alive again.

The tears were not a collapse but a rebirth, a reminder that feeling deeply is the doorway to living fully.

Shiva holds space. Shakti fills it with life. Without expression, there is no experience. Without Shakti, there is no creation. Together, they remind us that surrender is not about silence alone, but about allowing movement, voice, and emotion to flow without fear. Shakti teaches us that expansion is the soul's natural state — to feel, to express, to create, and to love without apology.

Energy Cleansing — Releasing What Doesn't Belong to You

We often carry energies that are not ours — past relationships, childhood conditioning, generational trauma, societal expectations. These burdens weigh down Shiva's stillness and destabilize Shakti's flow. Energy cleansing is essential for spiritual growth.

- **Breath cleansing:** Inhale deeply, hold, and exhale with intention: *"I release what is not mine."* Imagine dust leaving your aura.
- **Cordcutting visualization:** Picture the person or situation draining you. With a golden sword of Shiva's energy, cut the cord gently. Thank the experience and let it dissolve.
- **Water ritual:** Stand under a shower and imagine each drop washing away old emotions. Whisper softly: *"I return to myself."*

One person carried guilt from a past relationship for years, repeating the same patterns with every new partner. During a cordcutting meditation, they visualized letting go — not with anger, but with compassion. Tears flowed, but afterward came a lightness they hadn't felt in years. For the first time, they were free.

The spiritual lesson is simple: you cannot receive new energy while holding onto old wounds.

CHAPTER 9

(KARMIC THREADS AND SOUL LESSONS)

Relationships are not born only in this lifetime. They are continuations of bonds carried across lifetimes, woven by the subtle threads of karma. The soul remembers what the mind forgets, and this is why certain connections feel inexplicably strong, even when logic cannot explain them. A glance, a touch, or a single conversation can stir emotions that seem far deeper than the present moment. These are karmic connections — rooted in unfinished stories, carrying lessons that seek completion.

Sometimes these bonds arrive as blessings, offering comfort and familiarity, as though you have known the person forever. At other times, they appear as challenges, stirring conflict or pain that feels disproportionate to the situation. Yet both are purposeful. The soul does not measure relationships by ease or difficulty; it measures them by growth. A karmic partner may arrive to teach patience, forgiveness, or self-worth. Another may mirror wounds that still need healing. In this way, every encounter becomes part of the soul's curriculum, guiding us toward balance and wholeness.

To recognize a karmic thread is to see beyond the surface of the relationship. It is to understand that the intensity you feel is not random, but the echo of a deeper story. The lesson is not to cling to the past or to fear the bond, but to ask: *What is this connection teaching me? Where is it guiding my soul?* When we approach relationships with this awareness, even the most painful encounters transform into opportunities for awakening.

Karmic threads remind us that love, loss, joy, and struggle are never wasted. They are the soul's way of weaving wisdom across lifetimes. Each bond, whether lasting or fleeting, carries a lesson. And when we honour those lessons with gratitude, we release the weight of unfinished stories and step closer to freedom.

Imagine meeting someone and feeling instantly attached, even without logical reason. Spiritually, this is the soul recognizing unresolved karma. The connection may not last forever, but it exists to complete a lesson. When the bond ends, both souls feel lighter, as if released from an unseen weight.

Awakening Through Pain — Shakti's Fire

Pain is not punishment; it is awakening. Shakti uses fire to burn illusions, attachments, and stagnant energies. This is why spiritual growth often begins with heartbreak, loss, or endings. Pain forces us to confront truth, breaks the ego, reveals hidden wounds, and awakens dormant strength.

One person once lost a relationship they thought would last forever. The heartbreak shattered them, leaving months of grief and anger. Yet slowly, pain led them inward — into meditation, reflection, and healing. They discovered parts of themselves they had ignored for years. The pain did not destroy them; it brought them back to themselves.

When Shakti sets your life on fire, it is not to punish you, but to guide you toward your true path.

The Power of Silence — Shiva's Gift

In a world full of noise, silence becomes revolutionary. Silence is not emptiness; it is fullness. Shiva resides in silence, and when you sit in stillness, you meet the Divine Masculine within.

Silence calms the nervous system, reveals intuitive messages, softens emotional storms, and creates space for clarity. One person, overwhelmed by stress and responsibilities, began practicing just five minutes of silence each day. At first it felt uncomfortable, but soon they realized their heart knew answers before the mind. Silence became their sanctuary, a place where peace was always waiting.

Silence is Shiva's embrace — the doorway to higher wisdom.

The Sacred Purpose of Relationships

Relationships are spiritual contracts. Every person you meet plays a role in your awakening — some arrive to nurture, others to challenge, some to mirror your wounds, others to ignite growth, and a few to teach you the art of letting go. Each connection, whether fleeting or lifelong, carries a sacred purpose that extends beyond the surface of human interaction.

One person once believed their ex was the love of their life. The bond felt unshakable, and its ending seemed unbearable. Yet, in the quiet aftermath of heartbreak, clarity emerged. They realized the relationship had not been a mistake but a teacher. It had shown them the importance of self-worth, the necessity of boundaries, and the power of self-love. With these lessons integrated, their next relationship unfolded differently — calm, healthy, and aligned. They understood then that some people come to wake you up, while only a few are meant to walk beside you for the long journey.

Every relationship is part of the soul's evolution. Nothing is wasted, and nothing is accidental. Even the most painful encounters carry wisdom, shaping you into greater wholeness. To see relationships through this lens is to move beyond blame or regret and into gratitude. Each bond becomes a stepping stone, guiding you closer to your highest self.

When the Soul Becomes the Guru

There comes a point on the spiritual journey when external teachings, though valuable, no longer define you. They serve as guiding lights, but the real guru begins to rise from within. This is the awakening of inner Shiva — the voice of truth, silence, and wisdom that has always lived in the depths of your being.

The soul speaks in ways the mind cannot always explain. It guides through sudden clarity, deep knowing, intuitive warnings, and synchronicities that seem too precise to be coincidence. Its language is subtle yet undeniable. One person, torn about leaving a relationship, sat in silence searching for answers. In that stillness, a soft inner voice whispered: "You deserve peace." It was not loud or dramatic, but it carried the weight of truth. That gentle whisper became their guide, leading them toward a decision that honoured their soul's need for harmony.

The soul is the most honest teacher because it has no ego, only wisdom. Unlike the mind, which clings to fear and expectation, the soul offers clarity without judgment. It does not push or demand; it simply reveals. When we learn to trust this inner guru, surrender becomes natural. We stop chasing validation outside ourselves and begin to walk with confidence in the rhythm of our own truth.

To recognize the soul as guru is to realize that the answers you seek are not hidden in distant places or in the words of others. They are already within you, waiting to be heard in silence. This is the sacred lesson of karmic threads: while relationships and experiences shape us, the ultimate guidance comes from the soul itself. When you listen deeply, you discover that the path forward has always been illuminated from within.

The Sacred Power of Vulnerability

Vulnerability is not weakness; it is courage. It is the willingness to be seen in our raw truth, without masks or defences. Shakti flows through vulnerability, bringing emotion, openness, and authenticity, while Shiva strengthens it with presence, offering steadiness and safety. Together, they transform openness into power, turning what many fear into the very force that deepens connection.

One person spent much of their life hiding their feelings, convinced that emotions made them fragile. They bottled up their fears, their desires, even their joy, believing that silence was strength. Yet beneath the surface, isolation grew heavier. When they finally opened up to a friend about their struggles, expecting judgment, they were met instead with compassion and support. That moment changed everything. They realized that walls do not protect — they isolate. Vulnerability became their bridge to deeper connection, a doorway to intimacy and trust.

Shiva gives the strength to hold emotion without being overwhelmed. Shakti gives the courage to express it without shame. When these energies move together, vulnerability becomes sacred. It is the place where love is born, where healing begins, and where the soul learns that true power lies not in perfection but in authenticity. To surrender into vulnerability is to surrender into life itself — raw, real, and profoundly transformative.

The Alchemy of Heartbreak

Heartbreak is one of the most powerful catalysts for transformation. When the heart breaks, Shakti enters through the cracks, awakening emotions, intuition, and consciousness. Heartbreak dissolves illusions, forces introspection, reveals wounds, and redirects your path.

One person, shattered after a breakup, cried, reflected, and slowly rebuilt themselves. Months later, they realized they had become stronger, wiser, softer, and more self-aware. Heartbreak had not destroyed them; it dissolved the version of themselves that accepted less than they deserved.

Heartbreak is the universe pulling you out of the wrong story so you can enter the right one.

Past karma shapes present connections, but each bond — whether through pain, silence, destiny, vulnerability, or heartbreak — carries a lesson. Some souls come to heal, some to challenge, some to awaken, and some to free you. When you honour these karmic threads, you stop seeing relationships as accidents and begin to see them as sacred teachers.

CHAPTER 10

(SOUL CONTRACTS AND DIVINE ALIGNMENT)

Delays are not rejection; they are divine protection. They are the universe whispering, *"Wait. Not yet. It will make sense soon."* What feels like a pause is often a sacred alignment taking place beneath the surface. Energy may not yet be ready, circumstances may still be unfolding, or a better path may be waiting to reveal itself. The universe never truly says "no" — it says, *"right time, right place, right person, and right version of you."*

Consider the story of one person who longed for a promotion. They worked tirelessly, yet were repeatedly overlooked. Each rejection felt heavy, as though their worth was being dismissed. Months later, the role they had desired was eliminated during restructuring. Had they received it, they would have been trapped in instability. Instead, a far better opportunity appeared, one that matched their skills, values, and aspirations. What once felt like disappointment revealed itself as divine redirection. The delay revealed itself as protection, guiding them toward true alignment.

Delay is God's way of aligning destiny with readiness. It is the gentle reminder that timing is sacred, that every unfolding has its rhythm. When we surrender to this truth, frustration softens into trust. We begin to see delays not as obstacles but as guardians of our soul contracts, ensuring that what arrives is not only desired but destined. In this surrender, patience becomes faith, and faith becomes the bridge to divine alignment.

The Threshold of Transformation

Right before a major spiritual breakthrough, life often feels heavier. This heaviness is not punishment; it is purification. The universe does not test you to break you, but to strengthen your alignment. These challenges arrive as a way of clearing what no longer serves you, ensuring that when the blessing comes, you are ready to receive it fully.

Tests often appear when you are close to levelling up, when old patterns are dissolving, and when your intuition is awakening. It is the moment before dawn, when the night feels darkest. It is the pause before blessings arrive, when patience is stretched to its limit. These trials are not signs of failure but signals that transformation is near.

One person decided to heal their self-worth. They stopped chasing love and began honouring themselves, choosing to stand in the truth of their value. Almost immediately, someone from their past returned — a familiar figure who once mirrored their old wounds. This was not coincidence; it was a test. Would they fall back into the same patterns, or would they choose differently? This time, they listened to their soul. They honoured their growth, set boundaries, and refused to compromise their newfound strength. Within weeks, their emotional life transformed. The test had not been a trap, but an invitation to prove readiness.

Tests are simply the universe asking: *"Are you ready for what you asked for?"* They are the final threshold before breakthrough, the moment where your choices reveal whether you are aligned with the destiny you seek. When you meet these challenges with awareness and courage, you step into the next chapter of your soul contract, carrying wisdom that ensures your blessings are not fleeting but lasting.

Gratitude: The Key That Unlocks the Gate

Gratitude is one of the most potent spiritual forces. It has the power to shift your vibration instantly from scarcity to abundance. Every *thank you* becomes an offering to the universe, a subtle prayer that raises your frequency, softens fear, and opens the heart to receive. Gratitude is not simply a polite gesture; it is an energetic state that transforms the way you experience life.

One person once felt stuck and hopeless, weighed down by anxiety and convinced that nothing was working in their favour. A mentor gently suggested a simple practice: write down five things to be grateful for each day. At first, it felt mechanical, almost forced. But as the days passed, something began to change. Within weeks, their anxiety eased, their relationships improved, and unexpected opportunities appeared. Their external circumstances had not shifted overnight — but they had. Gratitude did not just change their mindset; it changed their frequency, aligning them with a flow of abundance that had always been available.

This is the sacred truth of gratitude: it expands your energy. It teaches you to see blessings where once you saw lack, to notice beauty where once you overlooked it, and to trust that even delays and challenges carry hidden gifts. Gratitude is the bridge between desire and manifestation, between fear and faith. When practiced consistently, it becomes more than a ritual; it becomes a way of living, a frequency that magnetizes joy, love, and divine alignment.

Remembering What Was Never Lost

Purpose is not discovered outside of you; it is remembered within. It is not something you chase in the world, but a return to your soul's original blueprint — the essence of who you have always been. You know you are remembering your purpose when you feel drawn to certain activities without explanation, when superficial pursuits lose their appeal, and when synchronicities begin to guide your path with gentle precision. These signs are not random; they are reminders from your soul, nudging you back toward alignment.

Purpose is always tied to the threads of your natural gifts, your emotional history, your wounds, your deepest joys, and ultimately, your service to the world. The very experiences that shaped you — the struggles, the triumphs, the passions that make your heart come alive — are all part of the design. Your purpose is not separate from your life; it is woven into it, waiting to be remembered.

One person worked diligently in a corporate job, meeting expectations yet feeling unfulfilled. Their days were structured, but their spirit felt empty. When they began painting again — something they had loved as a child — everything shifted. With each brushstroke, they felt alive, peaceful, and whole. It was not simply a hobby; it was their soul reminding them of who they truly are. In that moment, they realized that purpose is not about titles or achievements, but about resonance — the activities, expressions, and callings that awaken your inner truth.

Purpose is the echo of your soul calling you home. It is the quiet voice that says, *"This is who you are. This is what you came here to share."* When you listen, you discover that your purpose has never been lost. It has always been within you, waiting patiently to be remembered.

The Eternal Homecoming of the Soul

The ultimate goal of every spiritual journey is union — the reunion of your inner Shiva and Shakti. This sacred meeting is not abstract; it is the lived experience of emotional balance, inner peace, clarity, self-love, and higher consciousness. When these energies embrace within you, life begins to feel whole.

When Shiva and Shakti unite, the mind grows calm, no longer restless or consumed by endless questions. The heart becomes brave, willing to love without fear of rejection or loss. Intuition sharpens, guiding you with quiet certainty, and your energy becomes magnetic, drawing to you the people and opportunities that resonate with your truth. You stop chasing what was never meant for you and begin naturally attracting what is aligned. You stop fearing endings and begin trusting divine timing. You stop struggling for validation and begin resting in the fullness of your own worth.

After years of heartbreak and healing, one person finally touched this state of union. Their life was not perfect, yet within them was a deep inner silence. The storms of the past no longer defined them. Shiva was awake, offering clarity and stillness. Shakti was flowing, bringing vitality and joy. Together, they created balance. In that moment, they realized they had come home to themselves.

Union is not something to be found outside of you. It has always been within, waiting patiently for your awareness to rise high enough to feel it. Coming home to yourself is the recognition that you are already whole, already complete, already carrying the divine balance you seek. The reunion is not a destination but a remembrance — the soul's gentle return to its natural state of harmony.

The Soul's Contract — Why We Cross Paths

Not every person enters your life by accident. Some arrive because your souls made an agreement long before this lifetime. These sacred agreements — called soul contracts — are lessons, healings, and awakenings chosen by both souls to experience together. They are not random encounters but purposeful meetings, designed to shape your journey and guide your evolution.

Some contracts bring healing by triggering old wounds so they can finally be resolved. Others are karmic, balancing unfinished lessons carried forward from past lives. Some push you toward growth by challenging your comfort zones, while rare and precious ones reconnect you with love that has flowed across lifetimes. Each person carries a message. Each connection serves a purpose.

Imagine meeting someone who feels instantly familiar, as though you have known them forever. The bond is deep, undeniable, yet turbulent. At first, you may believe they are meant to stay forever. But later, with clarity, you realize they were not here to remain — they were here to teach. Their presence revealed lessons of self-worth, boundaries, and emotional strength. When the contract completes, the bond dissolves, but you are transformed. You carry forward the wisdom, even if the person is no longer by your side.

Do not regret the people you meet. They were written into your story before you were born. Every soul that crosses your path is part of the divine choreography of your life, guiding you closer to alignment with your highest self. When you begin to see relationships through the lens of soul contracts, you stop asking *"Why did this happen to me?"* and begin to understand *"This happened for me."* In that awareness, even heartbreak becomes sacred, and every encounter becomes a step toward wholeness.

The Divine Pause That Resets Destiny

Sometimes life halts your plans, slows your progress, or pauses relationships. This is not failure — it is protection. A divine pause is the universe's way of recalibrating your path, gently guiding you back into alignment when you have strayed too far into exhaustion, distraction, or imbalance.

Pauses arrive when your body is weary, your mind overwhelmed, or your soul longing for silence. They are not punishments but invitations — invitations to rest, to listen, and to rediscover the rhythm of your own being. In the stillness, clarity begins to surface. What once felt urgent loses its grip, and what truly matters begins to shine through. These pauses prepare you for something better, something more aligned with your highest self.

One person, after years of relentless stress and chaos, suddenly found themselves unable to continue their routine. At first, panic set in. They feared they were falling behind, that life was slipping away from them. Yet as the days unfolded, the pause revealed its hidden gift. In the quiet, they reconnected with themselves. Suppressed emotions rose to the surface and were finally healed. New interests emerged, passions long forgotten were rekindled, and a deeper sense of purpose began to take shape. What seemed like a breakdown was, in truth, a breakthrough. The pause was not a setback but a blessing — a spiritual reset.

When life slows you down, it is because your soul is trying to catch up with you. The divine pause reminds you that growth does not always happen in motion, sometimes it unfolds in stillness. In surrendering to the pause, you allow your soul to breathe, to heal, and to realign with the path that was always meant for you.

Authenticity — The Soul's Magnet

Your true power lies in authenticity. When you stop pretending, performing, or hiding emotions, your energy begins to radiate in its purest form. Authenticity is magnetic because it carries truth. Shiva represents that truth — the clarity and presence that grounds you. Shakti represents expression — the movement and voice that bring your inner reality into the world. When these energies unite, they create authenticity, a state where your being and your actions are in harmony.

Authenticity strengthens your aura, sharpens intuition, attracts relationships that are aligned, and brings emotional freedom. It is the invisible language your soul speaks before you utter a single word. People may not always understand why they feel drawn to you, but they sense the resonance of truth in your presence. When you are authentic, you no longer chase connection; you embody it.

One person lived for years behind a mask of confidence, carefully constructed to hide their insecurity. Outwardly, they seemed strong, but inside they battled constant self-doubt. The day they admitted their fears and opened up emotionally, everything shifted. Instead of judgment, they received compassion. Instead of distance, they found closeness. Their relationships deepened, and their energy began to heal. What they discovered was that vulnerability and authenticity are not liabilities — they are bridges to genuine connection.

Authenticity is your invitation for the universe to align your life with truth. It is the signal that says, *"I am ready to live as I truly am."* When you embody authenticity, you stop attracting situations that demand masks and start drawing experiences that honour your soul. In this way, authenticity becomes not only a personal liberation but also a spiritual magnet, pulling you into alignment with the life you were meant to live.

✅ Final Embrace — The Union Lives in You

This journey does not end with the final page. It begins anew within you. Every chapter you have read is not just philosophy or story — it is a mirror, reflecting the hidden brilliance of your own soul. Shiva and Shakti are not distant archetypes; they are the pulse of your breath, the fire in your heart, the silence in your mind.

Life will still test you. You will still stumble, grieve, and question. Yet now you know: every trial is a threshold, every pause a blessing, every encounter a contract written in the stars. Nothing is random. Nothing is wasted. The universe has been conspiring all along to bring you back to yourself.

Remember this: your purpose is not a treasure buried in the world — it is the flame already burning within. Your union is not something to chase — it is the wholeness that has always been yours. Your authenticity is not weakness — it is the magnet that draws truth to you.

So, when fear rises, breathe. When doubt whispers, listen deeper. When the world feels heavy, return to the dance of Shiva and Shakti within you. In that sacred rhythm, you will find balance, clarity, and love.

You are not becoming the union. ***You are the union.*** *You are the silence and the song, the stillness and the movement, the eternal homecoming of the soul.*